Poetry Four

Another Tapestry Of Words

Rona V Flynn

Thank you with all my heart
to those lovely people
who receive
my literary endeavours
with love.

Another Tapestry Of Words

Rona V Flynn

Index

Tied up with String

All I have to give you
is a handful of words
drawn together with string.
Fragrant, bitter,
sweet and light.
Woody, strong,
soft and wild.
Just a handful of words,
cut from the root
and tied up with ordinary string.

Rona V Flynn

Petrichor

Petrichor.
What a beautiful word.
Conjures up freshness
and vibrance of green.

Petrichor.
Sweet scent of the earth.
Unquantifiable.
Rain that has been.

Rona V Flynn

Secret Garden

There's a garden just beside a stream,
a sanctuary that's lush and green.
Wildlife flows where the garden grows
and treasures lie, by eye unseen.

It's filled with nature's artistry
with different greens for every tree.
A secret pool in the shadows' cool
hides frogs who venture wild and free.

Sun reflects on waters' ring
where round chicks bathe and blackbirds sing.
Gentle sounds trickle all around
like trails of stardust shimmering.

Blossoms scent the spring borne breeze.
Autumn fruits grow plump with ease.
Old wood twists where roses kiss,
bejewelled with butterflies and bees.

Linger for an hour or two.
Step and stone will lead you through,
past rainbow glass and soft tall grass
to Dingley Dell's sweet healing brew.

All is well in this garden fair,
Minds will ease relaxing there.
Hearts will swell, rapt by the spell
of nature's loveliness laid bare.

Rona V Flynn

Cider Apples

I hear the cider apples call.
Time comes soon they'll start to fall.
Be they large or be they small
we're going to make some cider.

Rosy greens of every hue
to crush and grind and pulp and brew.
Full of earthy fruity dew
to make some golden cider.

Sit by the fire and drink and sing.
What fun and laughter it will bring.
Pure and clear and sparkling
winter warming cider.

Wrapped up warm we'll wander free
to go Wassailing tree by tree
and spill the nectar liberally
to bless them for our cider.

Rona V Flynn

Threads of Clay

The day is long. Summer fills my eyes,
warming me with her smile.
Captivated, I sat for just a moment
but stayed a longer while.

Time tricks us, we barely notice
disappearing days.
In the merest blink, we turn to see
another time and place.

I rest beneath the shady boughs
where roots search strong and deep.
Embraced, I give of all I am
in sweet eternal sleep.

Rona V Flynn

By the Sea

When the sun is high and the weather's clear
a sunshine breeze blows right through here.
It's never still and there'll always be
some flowers swaying by the sea.

It's a pleasant breath that fills the soul.
Flotsam rids as minds unfold.
Spirits lift, faces smile
and we can see for miles and miles.

Rona V Flynn

Bleed Into the Walls

It takes time to bleed into the walls,
to be content and know a place is yours.
To feel you're not misplaced
in an unfamiliar space,
and to love the quirkiness and hidden flaws.

It's not yours until you've bled into the cracks
loves and hates and all that's in-between.
Your essence and your seed,
your longings and your needs,
your heart and soul and everything you've been.

Slowly, you will seep into the grain,
permeating atmosphere and mood.
Let every corner fill
with your being as you spill,
pouring freely as your inmost is renewed.

A warm welcome will be waiting there for you
like a friend whose arms are always open wide.
There will be comfort most of all
because you've bled into the walls and have a
home that's part of who you are inside.

Rona V Flynn

Colours of Love

She strolled along the pavement, smiling to those who
might see her.
Her face revealed a long history, sadness and joy
woven through the lines.
Pausing, she smiled at the old man.
He took another swig from his bottle.
Somewhere is his other shoe she thought, before
continuing to the bus stop.

The piercing scream jarred the air.
A young mother was at the end of her tether.
Large silent tears rolled down her little girl's cheeks.
"May I hold your baby?"
Without waiting, the old woman scooped up the
crying child from his buggy.
For a moment, the mother was stunned.
The little boy's screams soon stopped.
Soothed by gentle singing as the old woman rocked
him to and fro, his eyes began to close.
The floodgates opened.
As the mother sobbed, so too did her little girl.

The old woman lay the little boy in his buggy and passed her a handkerchief. "I have bread and cheese, and a large pot of tea waiting for me at home and no-one to share it with. Do you have half an hour to spare?"

Three hours later the young mother's eyes sparkled. She chatted away as she refilled their cups, and lively conversation continued.
The little girl, who the old woman now knew as Florence, sat on a worn rug, sharing her picnic with a very old teddy called Rumbletum, little Leonard lay fast asleep.

Their encounter was the beginning of a beautiful friendship.

Love comes in many colours.

Rona V Flynn

Glad Rags

Root out your Glad Rags
and put your lipstick on.
Those shoes in the back of the wardrobe
have been languishing too long.

We've watched and we have waited
through the hardest of our time,
but finally, the day has come
for sharing hugs and wine.

Put a new song on the jukebox,
let's dance and laugh and swing
to celebrate a new day
and the happiness it brings.

Rona V Flynn

Calming Camomile

Healing Words

Shed tears of sadness and
Open your heart.
Regret and
Remembering brings a new start.
Years of sorrow
can heal with one word
the deepest of wounds
and the pain of old hurt.
Today's the right time,
don't put off and wait.
Let's say sorry now
before it's too late…

Rona V Flynn

Little Bowls of Sunshine

Circle of gold, skipping and swaying
like Maypoling children laughing and playing.
Polished bowls of bright yellow sun
with stars breaking out
from the eye of each one.

They tumble and turn to song without word,
dancing to music and rhythm unheard.
Echoes of eons, times long gone,
and beautifully random
as time still to come.

Rona V Flynn

Liverpool Air

I saw Roger McGough
just the other day.
He stood beneath a spotlight.
He had a lot to say,
quoting poems and stories
from years well past and gone
when he used to be in 'Scaffold'
with his band mates Mike and John.
The arts scene was exciting then,
avant-garde and new.
Music and verse filled Liverpool air
at every rendezvous.

Rona V Flynn

Talking Heads

Sweet goodbye to heads on zoom
sitting in their living room.
Hello to arms spread wide for hugs
with touch and warmth
and screens unplugged.

Rona V Flynn

I've Been Here

I've been here once before in a dream,
I recognise this space.
I knew it looked familiar
when I saw that person's face.

The corridors are long and thin
and never seem to end.
Twists and turns lie everywhere,
they trick the mind and blend.

It seems I never find that
which constantly eludes
but wake to live another day,
reality renewed.

Rona V Flynn

Little Lizzie

Up before the dawn
to load her barrow full.
In all weathers, hail or snow,
sunshine bright or dull.

"Buy my flowers! Fresh today."
Crisp and clear and loud
her voice was heard six days a week
to echo through the crowd.

Her headscarf kept the wind at bay,
her shawl hugged close and warm.
Her image was familiar,
so well-known her tiny form.

From office boys to shop girls.
From scruff to fancy suit.
Everyone knew Lizzie
with her flowers and her fruit.

Clayton Square and Lewis's
for sixty years or more.
The oldest of twelve siblings
life was hard and they were poor.

Her rosy cheeks and friendly smile
will never be forgot.
Though life was tough, her heart of gold
lit up her barrow plot.

Rona V Flynn

Lizzie Christian
Liverpool Flower Seller
1898-1977

Middle Wood

There's a dell down there in Middle Wood
where shadows chase on every side.
High boughs loom and whisper low.
Every creak is magnified.
Ancient trees exude their tales.
through dampened air. Drawing near
they cloak you with their soothing spell,
pervading sense and atmosphere.

Rona V Flynn

The Man the Town Forgot

Wild, the ragged man, he raved,
wandering sad through friendless lanes.
Year on year he walked alone,
no door or hearth to call his own.

His face was weatherworn and lined,
his white hair long, his voice refined.
Pale blue eyes looked bright but cold,
his nails were long, his bones were old.

He doffed his hat and smiled anew,
begging for a coin or two.
His toothless grin showed much delight.
He disappeared into the night.

On he travelled, until the day
he knew at once *I've been this way.*
He looked along the cobbled street
with curtained windows nice and neat.

Children laughed and ran and played
until the light began to fade.
The wooden bench was strong yet old
and kept his cold bones from the road.

As he lay, he saw the clock
and memories came flooding back.
The joy, the pain, the sad farewell.
The ringing of the chapel bell.

His sun went out that dreadful day
and very soon, he lost his way,
wandering off into the night.
Thereafter was no sound, nor sight.

"Why is this old tramp sleeping here?"
The pompous Mayor was loud and clear.
"and what's he wearing on his feet!
He messes up our tidy street."

"But wait!" An old man stepped ahead.
"He looks so thin, first he'll be fed.
His coat is worn, his feet are sore.
I'll feed and clothe him, say no more."

But when they tried to rouse him there
he did not wake…he did not stir.
And when the man peered through the lines
he saw his friend from olden times.

"A friend of mine until the death
of his beloved left him bereft.
A gentle soul, so dear and true,
he fed the poor, no matter who."

Alone, the old man wept and sang.
The sun shone as the church bells rang.
"Take her to your breast dear friend,
your wretched torment has its end."

He knelt and laid forget-me-nots
in primrose yellow earthen pots
while blackbird poured out clear and long
his pure and lovely evensong.

Rona V Flynn

Beautiful forget-me-nots

Butterfly Blue

Butterfly blue
drifting gently in afternoon sun.
A silent scrap of perfection.
Violet shimmers catch the light,
fragile wings scatter blue.
Heartstrings sing.
Soul touched.

Rona V Flynn

January 2022

Blackest Nights

Winter brings the blackest nights
when clouded skies prevail,
but glimpses of a universe
peek through the misted veil.
Of planets, stars and galaxies,
comets, nebulae…
Of Saturn, Jupiter and Mars,
Venus, Mercury.
They slowly move and twist and spin,
turning in the deep,
held by the endless cloak of time
preserving cosmic sleep.

Rona V Flynn

Sweet Promise

Grass is much greener,
so they say,
in the garden
just across the way.
Its taste will be sweeter,
deliciously nice.
Oh the promise of pleasure,
all sugar and spice.

But sweet may be poison
and deadly to try,
leaving you broken
and hung out to dry.
For all of the time,
she over there
was secretly thinking
I wish I were her.

Rona V Flynn

Winter Haiku

Frost reflects bright light
sharp points twinkle in sunshine
cold ice warms the heart

Rona V Flynn

Always a Rainbow

Sunrise brings Red canopies,
Sunsets, Orange blaze.
Noon brings bright and Yellow sun.
Greens streak through the rays.

Azure brings us summer Blues
and picnics in the shade.
Dusk brings hazy Indigo
and Violet til it fades.

Even on our darkest nights
colours fill the skies
and far away, another place
wakes up to their sunrise.

Rona V Flynn

Raven

Your black shroud covered me
imprinting an image on my mind.
A fleeting glimpse of darkness,
too near to be.
Then you were gone.

Rona V Flynn

Just Life

Maybe the way through is difficult to see,
obscured by confusion and ambiguity.
This is a world that doesn't have a key
to navigate through life's uncertainty.

Living is something no-one can rehearse.
Learning as we go is a blessing and a curse.
Things get better, things get worse
because that's just life, and life is perverse.

Rona V Flynn

Drifting

Is there anything more tranquil
than a cruise beneath the skies,
following the waters
with the birds and dragonflies.

*Dozing lazy, drifting slow
through echoes of lives long ago.*

Folk are warm and friendly.
They wave and greet the day
amid the painted roses
of the pretty Sarah May.

*Shadows wait. From years long gone
the Lockmen watch as we roll on.*

Something in the summer air
carries on the breeze,
the scent of wild and nature
and time with friends at ease.

*Ghostly horses draw the line
along the tow-path, out of time...*

Cows amble idly
beside the waterway.
They turn to search our faces
as we travel through their day.

Rest at last for the boatman's friend
whose long days toil have reached their end.

We shared with one another
and picnicked in the sun,
enjoying time together
until the day was done.

Rona V Flynn

Drifting

Tomorrow

It's true to say
tomorrow never comes,
we chase it every day.
Today we never can enjoy
if it's always in the way.
When yesterdays are past and gone
then we will lament
on things we could have better done,
spurring discontent.
Enjoy today
when it arrives.
Bask and bathe in 'now'.
Appreciate and see and feel
the where, the who, the how.

Rona V Flynn

Black and White

Bustling pavements, cabs and busses.
Mobile-watchers blindly walk.
Laughing, shopping, drinking, eating.
People catching up to talk.

There's a buzz on the high street, sun is shining.
Busker's sing and catch your eye
hoping for a penny or few,
trusting you won't pass them by.

Sale-filled windows beg for custom.
We've got bargains, come and see.
Life and noise, excitement, chatter
fill the pavements vibrantly.

Darkness brings a different feel,
emptiness and people-bare.
Distant sounds seem so much nearer.
There's a staleness in the air.

Cats wail somewhere on a rooftop.
Windblown litter piles up deep.
Loud, the strange and eerie silence
of a busy town that sleeps.

Rona V Flynn

Magic

What is it that draws us together,
that peace when we don't need to try?
A glimpse of a heart that sees like ours,
never feeling we must explain why?

What unknown magic links us
with mysterious weavings unseen,
bringing laughter, fun and friendship
and calm in the spaces between.

That tangible sense of connection
that appears out of the blue.
These are the people to treasure
for we're sure to meet only a few.

Rona V Flynn

Sun Worshippers

Ragged and torn.
Windswept and blown.
Bowed heads laden
in gusts that are cold.
Leaves bedraggled,
withered and dry,
spent even more
as the days fly by.

But hope for the future
lies in the hearts
of golden sunshine
filled with new starts.
Again, they will stand up
tall and proud,
singing their song,
bright, happy and loud.

With smiles on their faces
they'll follow the sun
from dawn until dusk
when the silver is spun.

Rona V Flynn

Dawn

Warm breath disperses in cold dark air.
A soft glow spreads through dawn mist
as golden starlight breaks free.
Chilled wet stones come alive,
frosted grass twinkles.
Bright light devours scattering haze,
dazzling, intense, brilliant.
Rose, yellow, aqua spill across the sky.
The earth lies washed in a new day.

Rona V Flynn

Let it be for the good

If you remember me at all,
let it be for the good.
As someone who tried their imperfect best,
and failed to be all that I could.

Who endeavoured to have a kinder heart,
but often missed the mark,
who longed for a world that is fair and just
but saw far too much dark.

As someone who left too much undone
and wished she'd understood.
If you remember me for anything,
let it be for the good.

Rona V Flynn

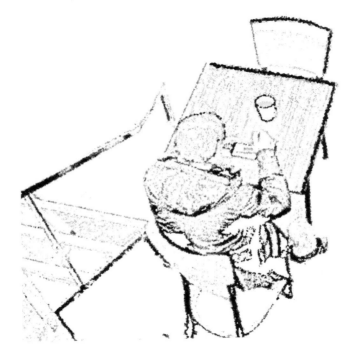

The Long Drink

Small table for one
next to the stairs.
A milky cup of tea.
Flicking through
old news
when there's nowhere else to be.

Rona V Flynn

Time for Turning

Tears of gold drift lightly,
brightened by evening sun.
Scarlet-splashed sweet honey
weeps for season gone.

Suspended mid dimension,
displacing fragile time,
gently, soft, they tip and fall
like fine spilled aging wine.

Rona V Flynn

Sisters

Morn adores the sunshine
chasing off the night.
She revels as it stretches out
to warm her with its light.

Noo will lounge in mid-day heat
and dream and loll and doze,
listening in the quiet
as time stops, unwinds and slows.

Eve smiles as twilight falls,
cool air kisses her cheek.
Shadows weave through all she sees,
playing hide and seek.

Nigh delights in deep blue skies
where bright stars glint and twink,
writing earth's long history
with interstellar ink.

Rona V Flynn

Blackout

When the lights went out all silence fell.
No chat and babble disturbing air
Just quiet and pitch black everywhere.

When the lights went out, came an icy chill.
No warmth or comfort or hot tea,
just waiting, cold and hopefully.

When the lights went out, the candle flame
made a bright and welcome warming glow
as shadows flickered to and fro.

When the lights went out the street went dark.
No lamps to light our way and guide.
No windows brightened from inside…

Then the lights came on and darkness fled.
Every room lit up as one.
Eerie shadows now were gone.
The gogglebox was loud and bright!
Windows shone into the night!
Lamplight pooled along the street!
My home was filled with LIFE and HEAT!
Parched and cold
it's time for me
to make a nice hot cup of tea.
I'm glad the lights are on.

Rona V Flynn

A nice cuppa to warm us up.

Sacking and Silk

Harsh times chafe and wear us down,
replacing joy with sorrow.
They make us sore and steal our smile
obscuring our tomorrow.
Dull and cold, rough to the touch,
cloaking us in dark.
Sunshine struggles to reach through
as sacking leaves its mark.

But oh, the silk of golden times,
the touch is soft and free.
Sun flows through translucent hues
with perfect clarity.
Feather light and smooth and kind,
ethereal and fine.
Warm and bright is the delight
that fills our happy times.

Rona V Flynn

Purple Paisley

Boots in purple paisley!
What more can I say?
Except they begged for rescue
from the treasure shop that day.

They fitted oh so perfectly,
delight for every toe.
But would I ever wear them?
I really didn't know…

Oh but when I look at them,
such colour and pizazz.
I can see them in the mirror
with their patterns and their jazz.

Alas, they've not yet ventured
into the light of day
and until I feel inspired
then it's home alone they stay.

My secret in the cupboard.
My hippy happy boots.
Seventies psychedelia
with flowerpower roots.

Rona V Flynn

Gertrude Jekyll Rose

Shapeshifter

It's a funny thing. We never know
when it will come, when it will go.
It just keeps changing all the time,
moving round and altering.
Suddenly we're faltering,
no reason or no rhyme.

A thought or memory brings a smile,
things forgotten for a while.
Then tripped we fall into the deep,
our heart is pierced for who we miss.
We want them here, not reminisce,
but now they are asleep.

The shape of grief, it alters so.
When it appears we just don't know
if it will bring a smile or tear.
Hovering, it's always there.
It brings us joy, it brings despair.
It brings them close and near.

Rona V Flynn

Bumblebees just love oregano flowers

Promise

Promise of spring whispers on the breeze.
Clear blue skies shower kisses.
Chills are warmed by morning sun.
Dark earth smiles and laughs in green.
Bony twigs fill and sprout.
The time for singing has begun.

Rona V Flynn

There will be
more than one little mouse hidden here.

Oh, To Be a Dormouse

Oh, to be a dormouse
playing in the sun.
I'd feast on seeds and hazelnuts
to fill my tiny tum.
Then I'd curl up for a big sleep
when all the world turned cold
and wake to warming sunshine
when earth and spring unfold.

Rona V Flynn

Be always kind
to your
body and mind

Morning Bliss

Chinks of morning sun
creep through slatted blinds.
Nestled in sleepy oblivion,
swathed in warmth and comfort.
Breath slow and deep,
drifting light as a feather
in dozy delight.

Rona V Flynn

On Parquet Floor

Tears fall to parquet floor,
the world slows to a stop.
Salted wounds bleed rhythmically,
drop by drop by drop.
Stains will last forever there,
indelibly ingrained.
Memory blended with old oak,
forever to remain.
A scrap of history sealed in time,
captured in the net
of life with its engravings of
those things we don't forget.

Rona V Flynn

Walk Gently

Walk gently in the lives of others.
Speak kindly when hearts are sore.
Have patience with those who try their best,
help them up when they hit the floor.

Let your smile be warm and accepting.
Speak soft when they've lost all hope.
Have compassion for those whose lives are hard
when they're trying their best to cope.

Remember to listen sincerely
so your heart can hear what they say,
and if you fail to stand when life gets tough,
find a friend who will walk your way.

Rona V Flynn

Scribed in Light

Cut down in her prime
in full flush of summertime,
she was a star of film and centre stage.

Hers was a brief chaotic life,
a beauty scribed in light,
an icon of the movie-making age.

Her youth will not decline
for we see skin still opaline
and lips and eyes
still sparkle on our screen.

We see pain and loneliness
behind the laughter and success.
We see a girl,
a hurt and broken Norma Jeane.

Rona V Flynn

Norma Jeane Mortenson ~ Marylin Monroe
1926 – 1962

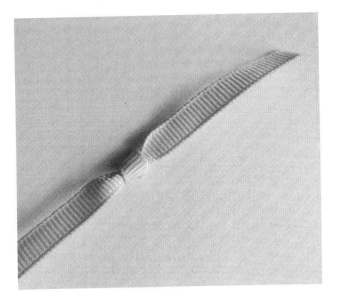

People Remember

People will remember how you made them feel.
May their memory tell them they were *Valued*.

People will remember how you made them feel.
Let them recall feeling always *Respected*.

People will remember how you made them feel.
May their heart warm, remembering *Acceptance*.

People will remember how you made them feel.
Let them smile and be glad when recollected.

People will always remember.

Rona V Flynn

A Lilacky Kind of a Day

It's a lilacky kind of a day,
calm, serene and easy.
Pastel clouds streak across the sky.
Warm air infused
with the breath of lilac
hangs close and heavy where I lie.

Skin against grass.
Cushioned by daisies,
cool, soft, and blissfully deep.
Senses sweetly heightened.
Body calmly resting,
floating to a dreamy, fragrant sleep.

Rona V Flynn

This and That

A little relaxation,
friendly conversation.
A little extra sharing,
tender love and caring.
Taking time for soothing,
unruffling and smoothing.
A little cosy snuggling,
less time for rush and juggling.
More giggling and clowning,
less grouchiness and frowning.
Time for reflection,
a little introspection.
Time to ponder and renew.
More of being true to you.

Rona V Flynn

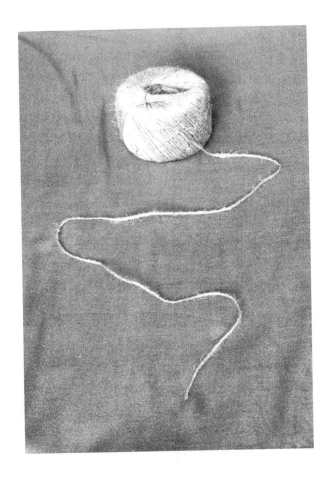

Just One Line

Just one line is all it takes
to lay a feeling down.
A memory, your heart's desire,
a thought of no renown.

A secret loosed upon a page
can ease a troubled mind.
Let creative juices flow
as deeper thoughts unwind.

A single sentence is a poem,
it's as long as a piece of string.
What's yours is yours and yours alone.
Rhyme or not is down to you.

Rona V Flynn

Close
Forgive
Welcome
Remember
Christmas Joy Letting Go Giving
Cheer Visit Embrace Talking Peace
Sharing Hope Dancing Invitations
Celebration Smiling Include Dance
Thanking Sincerity Friendship
Listen Reaching Out Grace
Hugging Noticing Gentle Stars
Joy Gifts Love Togetherness Sing
Happiness Generosity Waiting Gratitude
Meaning Hold Open Hearts Holding on
Kindness Patience Help Serve Love
Make Amends
Laughter
Talking
Forget
Rest

Rona V Flynn/Facebook/Amazon

90

What d'you want for Christmas

What d'you want for Christmas?
This year it's for free.
Expensive presents will not show
the love inside of me.
Face to face and talking,
touch and eye to eye.
We won't find a fancy shop
for gifts we cannot buy.

Rona V Flynn

Old Father Time

Long white hair and wizened face.
Rickety old legs slow his pace.
Tattered white beard sweeps the ground,
frayed and tangled, knotted round.
His eyes are misted, he's lost his glow.
It's almost time for him to go.

The wintery winds swept him away
in a whistling flash. It's New Year's Day!
The Old is gone, the New is here
to create fresh memories.

Happy New Year.

Rona V Flynn

I'd love to hear from you.

Well, there we are...

...my fourth book of poetry, I hope you enjoyed reading it as much as I enjoyed writing it.

This one took a little longer with almost two years of COVID and isolation. I did find it a bit of struggle, I'm sure you probably did too.

Anyway, later than I had planned it is finally here. The year 2022 is hopefully a healthier and happier year for all of us.

So while we still have the chance…

Let's be kind to one another and keep in touch with those who are precious.

Rona x

Please turn the page for information about other books.

Snippets of Reviews
for this and previous publications

Poetry Books One to Four

Bleed into the Walls
Great poem, great title.
I never thought of it like that.

Sacking and Silk
I've been there!

Wild Wood
"I love the peace and tranquillity of this poem.

People will always Remember
So true.

Long Love
A beautiful poem with echoes of Greek myths.

Daydream
This poem is so true.
It's very wordy which I think that compliments the almost
'nothingness' of daydreaming. It's so effortless yet there's so
much going on with daydreaming,

Low light in September
I LOVE Low Light in September. It's so evocative of crisp,
cold autumn.

Damsels and Dragons
"What a beautiful poem. So full of wonderful imagery. The process is pretty amazing and the author has captured the magic and mystery very descriptively." Nature Lover.
The British Dragonfly Society liked this poem so much that they shared it on their Facebook Page.

Blackbird
"The poem entitled 'Blackbird' is beautiful and I love the author's description of its song. It is such a magical sound and she expresses it so perfectly. I also like the blackbird's eye being 'starlight cloaked in ebony velvet.' Gorgeous!"
Lesley Rawlinson, Author.

Earth's Bones

"The author shows great insight into the Earth's amazing processes in the poem 'Earth's Bones'. I love it!"
Jennifer Jones, Earth Scientist and Author.

"Some very emotive poems sparking memories; contemplation; some smiles and some sadness."
"Beautiful and sometimes poignant."
"I really like this author's poems.
She has a subtle use of language."
"Some poems have a spiritual feel."
"Insightful, the Author is reading my mind!"

Silver Key

"You will not be disappointed with this next book of The Light Keepers series! I absolutely loved it and was moved to tears in some parts and laughing out loud in others."

"Star's journey took us through magical portals, and introduced an array of new and interesting characters, including a couple on the dark side.

"I can't wait for the next book now, I loved reading about the struggle between darkness and light and the inner struggles of the characters. It so true to life!"

"An enjoyable story, with a hint of a new adventure to come."

"They are absolutely brilliant books! I couldn't put them down as I was so excited to find out what happens next. I can't wait until my daughter is old enough to read them, I know she's going to love them."

Star's Awakening

"The author has created a really vivid world. The book is easy to read and nicely paced."

"I thoroughly enjoyed it. It was one of those books I just wanted to keep on turning the pages to find out what was happening next."

"I thoroughly enjoyed this book. The characters were easy to visualise."

"A good story line and great characterisation."

"I was totally drawn into the life of the central family."

"It was amazing. I absolutely loved the story line and the characters!! Can't wait for the next book in the series."

"An interesting and enjoyable read, I was drawn into the story right from the beginning."

"I was intrigued, it was complex, I couldn't put it down."

Cont'd…

My novels are available on Kindle and in paperback

Two stories with just a touch of fantasy. These tales follow Star and her family through the twists and turns of family life as she becomes an adult. Old secrets are uncovered and new friends and enemies are made as their journey unfolds.

Star's Awakening and The Silver Key feature the age-old struggle between good and evil, and the family's journey through it. The tales begin in Gawswood, a close-knit community with Star's family is at the heart of it.

Star's Awakening – Lightkeepers Book One
Star's widowed father is the settle Elder. All is well, but as Star prepares for her coming of age, everything begins to change. Old enemies, the discovery of family secrets, and life-changing events lead us through their journey.

The Silver Key – Lightkeepers Book Two
The continuation of *Star's Awakening* picks up the family's tale five years later. Life in Gawswood has been good - but all is not as it seems. We watch the human condition weaving its way through the trials and tribulations that beset them. Interesting new characters join them as they search for answers and closure.

Thank you
x